Personal Finance 101
Canada's Housing Market Analysis
Buying vs Renting a Home

Personal Finance 101
Canada's Housing Market Analysis
Buying vs Renting a Home

A Case Study

Dmitry Newman

Library of Congress Control Number: 2016901455
ISBN: Hardcover   978-1-5144-5475-6
               Softcover   978-1-5144-5474-9
               eBook   978-1-5144-5473-2

Print information available on the last page.

Rev. date: 01/28/2016

To order additional copies of this book, contact:
Xlibris
1-888-795-4274
www.Xlibris.com
Orders@Xlibris.com
732449

CONTENTS

What you will find in this book:

- A case study that examines a real-life "buy" versus "rent" option available for a Canadian household.

- Tools to assess your financial position to make an optimal decision either to buy or to rent a home.

- Analysis of Canada's real estate market and its growth prospects using jargon-free nontechnical language.

Housing Market Environment Overview

P erhaps one of the most important personal finance decisions made by a family in their lifetime is whether to buy or to rent a home. Shelter costs generally exceed a third of a disposable income, and a decision to buy a home can make a family wealthy due to excessive capital gains or result in a nightmare if the housing market undergoes a price correction.

A large number of American homeowners earned hefty profits by investing money in real estate and flipping homes in the early 2000s. By the same token, there was a large number of households that lost fortunes and fell into a multiyear debt trap during the 2008–09 financial crisis when the national average house prices plummeted by more than 20 percent in just four years (from its peak in January 2008 to the trough in December 2011).[1]

Many homeowners were forced into a foreclosure after losing a job and found themselves in a so-called deep underwater mortgage situation (when the current market value of the house is less than the purchase price). To date, housing market prices in the United States were not able to fully recover and remain roughly 10 percent below the peak price level achieved in 2008, as illustrated in chart 1.

---

[1]   Standards & Poor's Dow Jones Indices McGraw Hill Financial, "S&P/Case-Shiller Home Price Indices," retrieved August 10, 2015, from Haver Analytics database (CASUSXAM@USECON; CASC20XA@USECON; CASCSXA@USECON).

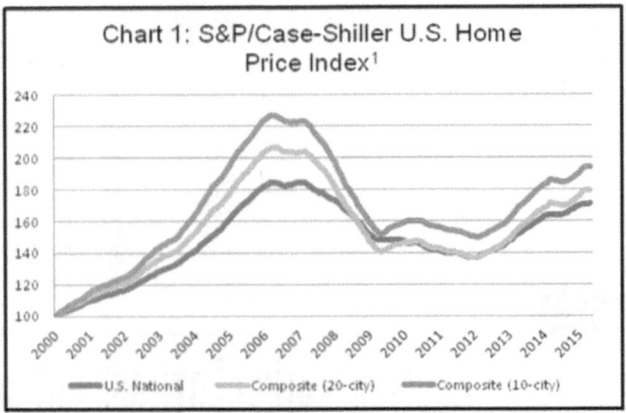

Chart 1: S&P/Case-Shiller U.S. Home Price Index[1]

Despite such a disastrous outcome from the housing bubble burst in the United States and a worldwide economic meltdown, the housing sector in Canada was only briefly impacted by the financial crisis as home prices declined by 8 percent and returned to the prerecessionary price level by the end of 2009.[2] Afterward, the growth was continued, and since then, we are seeing home prices beating record highs month-after-month, as illustrated in chart 2.

The big question is how sustainable this price growth trend is. Section 3 of this book outlines forces of supply and demand that influenced the market in recent years and provides some insight on future growth prospects of home prices in Canada.

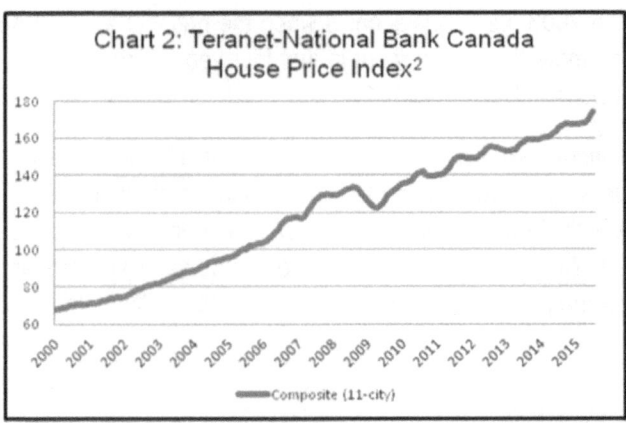

Chart 2: Teranet-National Bank Canada House Price Index[2]

---

[2]   Teranet and National Bank of Canada, "Teranet – National Bank National Composite House Price Index," retrieved August 10, 2015, from Haver Analytics database T11I@CANADA.

One might wonder what caused such a difference between housing markets in Canada and its southern neighbor. The answer is quite simple.

For one, there was no housing bubble in Canada at the verge of the economic crisis to begin with, while the US housing market was overheated by subprime mortgage lending (i.e., lending to households with poor credit ratings). On the other hand, housing in Canada was fairly priced, and conservative lending practices were taking place.

Currently, only around 5 percent of Canada's mortgages are subprime, compared with nearly 25 percent of America's mortgage loans before the market crash. Moreover, two-thirds of mortgages are insured by the federal body, Canada Mortgage and Housing Association, or one of its private competitors, which offers some degree of protection to lending institutions in Canada.[3]

Secondly, Canada's economy and financial system proved to be more sustainable than America's. As a result, the Canadian labor market experienced growth shortly after the recession, and a home buying activity resumed quickly, which prevented the housing market from being flooded with foreclosures.

In recent years, however, the tables might have turned.

America's economy exhibits signs of growth acceleration that surpass Canada's economy that was hit hard by the slump in oil prices (natural resources sector accounts for roughly 20 percent of the economy in Canada). The province of Alberta, especially felt the impact of the plunge in the oil prices. For the period from October 2014 to October 2015, the unemployment level skyrocketed by 2.2 percent from 4.4 percent to 6.6 percent (while the national unemployment level increased by 0.4 percent to 7.0 percent).[4]

The disturbance in Alberta's labor market had a tremendous impact on the housing market in the province, as Calgary housing sales plunged 33 percent with a decline in the average price by 6 percent. [5]

---

[3]   The Economist, "Late to the Party" (October 17, 2015), 44.

[4]   Statistics Canada, *Table 282-0087 - Labour Force Survey Estimates (LFS) by Sex and Age Group, Seasonally Adjusted and Unadjusted, Monthly (Persons Unless Otherwise Noted)*, CANSIM database, accessed November 20, 2015.

[5]   Calgary Real Estate Board, *Calgary Regional Housing Market Statistics* (October 2015), available from http://www.creb.com/~/media/Public/CREBcom/Statistics_Package/2015/October_2015.pdf.

On the national level, a year-over-year increase in housing prices in October 2015 was 8.3 percent, but excluding the bubbly areas of Greater Vancouver and Greater Toronto, the national price increase was a modest 2.5 percent,[6] according to the Canadian Real Estate Association.

With the deterioration in the housing market in Alberta that might spread to other provinces (if the negative trend in the oil industry persists), more and more global investors are placing bets on a drastic decline in housing prices and the negative impact on mortgage lenders.

The Markit research reported a growing number in foreign investors taking "short" positions (positions that become profitable on a price decline of the underlying securities) on Canadian lenders,[7] which essentially places a bet on a meltdown of the housing market, inability to pay mortgage obligations by homeowners, unsustainable write-offs by the lenders, and a freeze in mortgage lending.

In the summer/fall of 2015, Home Capital Group (a lending institution primarily tailored for prospective homeowners that were turned down by larger lenders and which is considered a proxy for Ontario housing market, given the company's high exposure to the bubbly housing market in Toronto) experienced a sharp increase in "short" positions and was named as the most shorted financial institution in Canada based on the expectations of a substantial plunge in housing prices that will cause a spike in foreclosures and force the company into a bankruptcy.[8]

Given the stability of Canada's financial system, a mortgage insurance requirement for loans with a down payment of under 20 percent, the degree of government regulations, the conservative approach, and the size of the major lenders, it might be hard to believe that a housing market price correction and a rise in foreclosures can potentially cause a meltdown of the Canadian financial system, but small lenders might certainly be at more risk (the "too big to fail" concept might not be applicable to such institutions).

---

6   Calgary Real Estate Board, *Calgary Regional Housing Market Statistics* (October 2015), available from http://www.creb.com/~/media/Public/CREBcom/Statistics_Package/2015/October_2015.pdf.

7   Kalyeena Makortoff, "Why Investors Are Shorting Canada's Housing Market," CNBC (October 30, 2015), accessed November 20, 2015, available from http://www.cnbc.com/2015/10/30/why-investors-are-shorting-canadas-housing-market.html.

8   Kalyeena Makortoff, "Why Investors Are Shorting Canada's Housing Market," CNBC (October 30, 2015), accessed November 20, 2015, available from http://www.cnbc.com/2015/10/30/why-investors-are-shorting-canadas-housing-market.html.

By no means such a pessimistic look by foreign investors should be considered a sole reason for a housing market price correction in Canada, but such an investment vehicle as "shorting" (especially in a foreign market) is generally utilized by professional investors with a clear outlook and opinion rather than casual amateur investors, and most certainly such an outlook by these investors on the housing market in Canada should be included in our "worry list."

For instance, a more apparent and concerning issue is the unprecedented level of household indebtedness.

Record-high indebtedness level of the Canadian households with the debt-to-income ratio at 167 percent in the second quarter of 2015[9] makes households and the overall housing market most vulnerable to macroeconomic and labor market shocks since most of the borrowing has gone into buying houses, resulting in overheating of the market. This trend is compared to the deleveraging cycle in the United States where the debt-to-income ratio for households improved dramatically since its peak in 2007.

The survey conducted by the Manulife Bank in the spring of 2015 determined that more than 40 percent of Canada's homeowners would have difficulty making regular mortgage payments within only three months if the primary income earner lost their job.

A more worrisome finding from the survey is that more than a third of homeowners would have difficulties making monthly mortgage payments after a 10 percent increase in payment and 15 percent of the respondents would not be able to absorb any increase in payments.[10]

The Bank of Canada overnight interest rate (a rate that directly influences mortgage rates set by lending institutions in Canada) at 0.50 percent at the time of writing is near its record-low level, which resulted in the five-year fixed mortgage rate declining to its record-low level in the summer of 2015.

Households buying homes and locking into the most popular conventional five-year fixed rate mortgage term in 2016 will have an assurance of paying low interest, but since an amortization period of the loan is long-term in nature (usually twenty

---

9   Statistics Canada, *Table 378-0123 - National Balance Sheet Accounts, financial indicators, households and non-profit institutions serving households, quarterly (percent)*, CANSIM database, accessed November 25, 2015.

10   Manulife Bank, *Homeowner Debt Survey* (Spring 2015), 8–9.

to twenty-five years), the renewal of the mortgage loan in 2021 might potentially be done under different interest rate terms, and most likely, a higher interest rate.

The current Bank of Canada rate is more on the abnormal than normal side as a result of implementation of loose monetary policy addressing a worldwide economic meltdown from one of the most difficult financial crises since the Great Depression. The Bank of Canada cut the rates from 4.50 percent in the fall of 2007 to 0.25 percent in the spring of 2009,[11] resulting in a rapid decline of the five-year conventional mortgage lending rates from 6.8 percent to 4.8 percent during the same period and a more gradual decline of the rate to the historically lowest level of 3.7 percent in the summer of 2015.[12]

Note that mortgage rates did not decline instantaneously to the lowest level in 2008 despite the near-zero overnight rate due to other factors that influence mortgage lenders in setting their rates, such as elevation of default prospects on mortgage loans and general economic conditions. However, under normal economic conditions, most of the decline/increase in the Bank of Canada overnight rates is almost fully translated to mortgage rates.

The tendency of interest rate cuts implemented by central banks as a measure of addressing the worldwide economic recession was common among all advanced economies. Since 2008, the growth of world GDP normalized (although it is far from the prerecessionary levels, but the double-digit growth of the Chinese economy is behind us, and the current global growth in low single-digits is considered acceptable by many), resulting in a desire by some central bankers to set a policy normalization cycle as abnormally low interest rates cause certain dangers for monetary policy instruments and the overall safety of an economy.

For instance, the Federal Reserve of the United States is expected to start policy-normalization cycle (i.e., overnight interest rates increases) in late 2015/early 2016, causing mortgage rates to follow suit.

However, interest rate increases in Canada will be postponed. The Canadian economy was highly negatively affected by the decline in oil prices that put the country in a technical recession in the first half of 2015, which forced the Bank

---

[11] Bank of Canada, *Overnight Money Market Financing Rate*, retrieved August 15, 2015, from Haver Analytics (B156RD@CANADA).

[12] Canada Mortgage and Housing Corporation, *Conventional Mortgage Lending Rate: Five-Year Term* retrieved August 15, 2015 from Haver Analytics (DP00001@CANADA).

of Canada to implement two additional interest rate cuts from 1.0 percent at the beginning of 2015 to 0.50 percent in the summer of 2015.

But the actions of monetary policy officials from south of the border indicate that the abnormally low rates are not a new norm and that the rates will be increased as soon as there is certainty that a rise will not cause a new recession and that the impact of the decline in oil prices in Canada is weakened.

A simple calculation indicates that if the five-year mortgage rates are returned to the prerecessionary level of 6.8 percent from the current 3.7 percent, monthly mortgage payments are expected to increase by over 35 percent, which most certainly will impose difficulties for middle-class households that allocate more than 50 percent of their disposable income on house-related expenses.

On the other hand, renters are protected by provincial Residential Tenancies Act that to some extent shelter tenants from rapid and unjustified rent increases, as opposed to homeowners who essentially are on their own once the time of mortgage renewal comes and the interest rates are doubled.

A careful assessment of an ability of a household to absorb potential mortgage payment increases by 25 to 30 percent throughout the duration of the loan is highly important for prospective homeowners. This is most relevant for households that are struggling to make a minimum 5 percent down payment.

The Canadian Association of Accredited Mortgage Professionals estimated that 26 percent of first-time homebuyers (which translates to 14 percent of all mortgage loans) raise a down payment through the means of gifts from relatives or loans.[13] This worrisome result should raise concerns among prospective homeowners, as well as the federal authorities.

And it seems that the government has started taking small careful steps in the direction of market interventions.

On December 11, 2015, the new finance minister, Bill Morneau (that assumed the office just over a month prior to this) announced fairly radical changes to the down payment requirements that will take effect in February of 2016.

For properties priced under $1 million, the minimum down payment requirement was a flat 5 percent rate in order to qualify for mandatory mortgage insurance. With

---

13   Veritas Investment Research, *Canadian Housing Market Update* (June 26, 2015), 9.

the changes, the minimum down payment requirement increased to 10 percent for the amount above $500,000 and for the portion under $500,000, the rate was kept unchanged at 5 percent.

For instance, a $750,000 house will now require a minimum down payment of $50,000, compared to $37,500 previously.

Homes priced over $1 million are not affected by the changes as the minimum down payment of 20 percent is required for these properties, and as such, no mortgage insurance requirement is imposed.

Some analysts estimate that the changes will only affect a small number of buyers who will only need a few extra months to save up money to fulfill the new requirement and enter the market regardless of the changes.

A nearly universal opinion among pundits is that these changes will not have any drastic impact on house prices in Canada as there will be no impact on the demand. However, a single most important conclusion I could draw from this announcement is a change in the perception of the housing market by the federal authorities, who have all the necessary tools to cool down the market more drastically if the overheating continues.

It is important to recognize that the government no longer monitors the trends in the housing market but rather introduces new measures that have a direct impact on the housing market in Canada.

Another important point is that this is a newly elected Liberal government and one of the first moves by the Ministry of Finance was an intervention in the hosting market. The new minimum down payment requirement is arguably the strongest government intervention, compared to anything introduced by the Conservative government in the last decade. And the new Liberal government is in power at least until 2019.

This new requirement will most likely be on the unpopular side of government initiatives, but it is a much-needed one as it provides a necessary signal to the market participants that the recent trends in the housing market are more on the abnormal side and that the homeownership rate is not a number one priority for the government.

Some families consider homeownership as a certain social superiority and homeownership rate is quoted by many publicists as the single most important factor in determining society's financial health and stability. While there is no question that each and every single family should have a roof over their heads, a placement of homeowners over home renters on a social ladder and a desire for as many households as possible to own a home rather than to rent is a mistake.

In Europe, for instance, the highest homeownership rates are seen in Romania, Lithuania, and Slovakia (95.6 percent, 92.2 percent and 90.5 percent, respectively) and Greece has a rate of 75.8 percent. While the lowest homeownership rates in Europe are in Germany (52.6 percent) and Switzerland (44 percent).[14]

On the other hand, GDP per capita in Romania (a country with more than double Germany's homeownership rate) is nearly five times lower than in Germany.[15] It is not worthwhile to provide a lengthy discussion on the quality of life and the level of economic development in Romania relative to Germany and Switzerland—it should be evident enough.

Moreover, the homeownership rate in the United States swelled to the level of 69 percent in 2004, which was caused by an increase in homeownership rate by low-income families that could not afford to own a house, as well as aggressive subprime lending practices. After the bubble burst in 2008, the rate declined to around 64 percent[16] which is not indicative of a decline in prosperity of American households in 2015 relative to 2005.

These examples illustrate that homeownership is not necessarily a symbol of prosperity and is not always optimal for a family. One of the worst decisions a family can make is to purchase something it cannot afford, especially a purchase that is equal to ten-plus years worth of disposable income.

The most socially responsible thing a government can do is to promote affordable housing rather than to encourage homeownership, especially in an overheated market.

---

[14]   Alan Freeman, *Harper Is Playing Politics with a Housing Bubble Ready to Pop.* (iPolitics, October 9, 2015), accessed November 10, 2015, available from http://ipolitics.ca/2015/10/09/harper-is-playing-politics-with-a-housing-bubble-ready-to-pop/.

[15]   The World Bank, *GDP per Capita (Current US$)*, accessed November 5, 2015, available from http://data.worldbank.org/indicator/NY.GDP.PCAP.CD.

[16]   US Census Bureau, *Current Population Survey/Housing Vacancy Survey, Series H-111*, accessed December 5, 2015.

According to The Economist, Canada's housing is 34 percent overvalued against disposable income (relative to the long-term average), and compared with rents, the overvaluation is 89 percent.[17] A purchase of overvalued housing by low-income families carries economical risks and might cause shortfalls in government finances that can take generations to fulfill.

Many believe that overheating of the housing market was caused by foreign demand (especially this is evident in Toronto and Vancouver that saw a spike in inflow of foreigners in recent years and experienced the highest growth rates in home price levels), but there are no regular official data sources on foreign ownership rates that could provide a clear picture of the impact of foreign buying on home prices in Canada.

The only attempt by the government authorities was a CMHC survey of foreign ownership of condominiums conducted in the fall of 2014 and 2015. The survey determined that foreign ownership of condominiums was insignificant but exhibited statistically significant growth over the period from the fall of 2014 to the fall of 2015—Toronto foreign ownership rose from 2.4 percent to 3.3 percent, and in Vancouver, the increase was from 2.3 percent to 3.5 percent.[18]

These findings provide a certain relief and understanding that foreign demand does not control most of the buying activity in Canada, which is quite comforting and assuring that deterioration in foreign economic conditions or policy changes should not have a direct and a sharply negative impact on Canada's housing market. However, the report does not provide any data on house ownership, which might draw a completely different picture than the data on condo ownership share by foreigners. In addition, there is no mentioning of the share of Canada's newcomers in the housing market.

In my opinion, the most important segment of homebuyers that should be carefully monitored is the share of new immigrants buying homes in Canada. Each year, the country welcomes over 250,000 immigrants, and it is evident that the implementation of new stringent immigration laws will have an adverse impact on the inflow of new immigrants, which in turn should have a negative impact on demand for housing (a discussion on the topic of immigration is to follow in the last section of the book).

---

[17]   The Economist, "Late to the Party" (October 17, 2015), 44.

[18]   Tamsin McMahon, *More Foreign Buyers Snapping up Canadian Condos: CMHC* (The Globe and Mail: December 3, 2015), accessed December 5, 2015, available from http://www.theglobeandmail.com/report-on-business/economy/housing/the-real-estate-beat/foreign-buyers-target-canadas-condo-market/article27579550/.

Every young Canadian family out there is evaluating their options and possibly dreaming of entering the housing market in the capacity of an owner, but there are some important questions that you might want to ask yourself before proceeding:

- Will capital appreciation (if any) in the long run be sufficient to compensate for all the additional expenses associated with homeownership?

- Can we actually afford to buy a house at current prices?

- What are the risks involved in owning a house as opposed to renting?

- Are we able to sustain an increase in mortgage payments that is likely to occur throughout the duration of the mortgage loan?

The goal of this book is to try to answer all these questions and equip a reader with tools that will enable him/her to carefully assess the market conditions and decide on whether it makes any sense to enter the market.

At all times, I try my best to avoid technical jargons and to ensure that readers with no finance background are able to understand the concepts, follow the intuition behind my housing market forecast, and finally, apply the tools to evaluate their own financial position.

A Numerical Case Study

I n this section of the book, I provide an evaluation of two options for a household— buying versus renting a real house available for sale/rent in Toronto. The tool developed for this section can be applied by the readers to evaluate their own "buy" versus "rent" options.

The main goal of this book (and this section in particular) is to assist families in a careful evaluation of their options. There is nothing wrong in making a conclusion that renting at the present time is the most optimal option and that the homeownership goal should be postponed for another five to ten years when the real estate market is more reasonably priced, the growth potential for housing prices is more certain, and when a stable career and the family financial position is stronger.

Buying and flipping houses can certainly be a good business and a good way to earn a hefty profit (as was seen in the United States in the early 2000s and in Canada in the last five years), but as the third part of the book demonstrates, current market conditions impose elevated risks on this business strategy. Even if the goal of homeownership is pure ownership of a roof over your head (not a "buying and flipping" strategy), the points and examples highlighted in this book illustrate the obstacles, costs, and difficulties of entering the market at the present time.

Before calculations are presented, it might be useful for readers to understand the costs/risks to be incurred by a homeowner and the assumptions used in the calculations:

Mortgage Broker's Fees/Commission

Many first-time homebuyers are only mildly aware of the costs associated with owning a house. Although mortgage broker's fees are generally paid by sellers, at some point in your lifetime, these costs will be incurred by your household if you choose to buy a house at a young age and end up selling it in five to ten years.

These costs are measured in tens of thousands of dollars (brokerage fees are generally equal to 5 percent of the sale price), and when buying a second house, many tax credits will no longer be available (for example, land transfer tax rebate is only available for first-time homebuyers).

In addition, a buyer most often incurs legal and appraisal fees at the time of purchase, which amounts to thousands of dollars and are not included in the list price.

Taxes

When buying a home, a buyer is responsible for paying land transfer tax. Depending on the location of the house/condo, both provincial and municipal land transfer taxes are applicable.

The range of the tax is anywhere between 1 percent and 4 percent of sale price, depending on price and location of the property. We will not get into the discussion of the structure of the tax as there are many convenient calculators available online that enable buyers to estimate the amount of the tax.

Aside from the land transfer tax, a homeowner is faced with annual property taxes, which depend on the location and the neighborhood of the property.

Maintenance Fees

Maintenance fee is another major expense that is usually covered by landlords.

The amount of maintenance fees for a 1,000-square-feet condo alone are equal to an all-inclusive rental price of a modest bachelor unit, of course, depending on the amenities offered in the units. It is in the best interest of families to evaluate each possible option available for comfortable living.

A worrisome issue is the way the new condo buildings (e.g., glass exterior) are constructed, and more and more analysts express concerns over the possibility that maintenance costs for these buildings might drastically increase.

If a newly built condo unit has a modest maintenance cost of $0.50 per square foot, within ten years this cost might increase to $0.80 per square foot, depending on the issues that arise with the aging building. This increase translates to an extra $3,600 per year spent on maintenance costs for a 1,000-square-feet unit.

Capital Renovation Costs

In addition, a homeowner absorbs the risks associated with capital renovations of the property, whereas a tenant avoids these risks as these costs are a responsibility of the landlord, and a tenant is protected under the provincial Residential Tenancies Act.

Forgone Earnings on a Down Payment

When making a down payment, a buyer is essentially giving up an opportunity to earn income on that amount elsewhere. Nowadays, any big bank offers direct investment accounts, along with recently introduced Tax-Free Savings Accounts (TFSA). These tools enable families to make investments and earn tax-free income and with a minimal amount of commissions.

A wide array of inexpensive and highly liquid passive investment vehicles (such as mutual funds and exchange-traded funds) is available for investors that do not have the essential knowledge of portfolio construction and can simply make an investment (shares or bonds traded anywhere in the world), and have an option to place and execute a trade within a few minutes in the comfort of their own home, using online banking services.

For simplicity, the model assumes a 5 percent per year forgone earnings on the amount of the down payment (this rate is also embedded in the spreadsheet that is available to the readers).

Insurance Costs

In addition to substantial, and at times unpredictable, expenses incurred by a homeowner, there is also a large number of smaller expenses such as mortgage insurance that is required to be purchased by a buyer who makes a down payment smaller than 20 percent of the purchase price (the biggest provider is the government Canada Mortgage and Housing Corporation) and is equal to $30 to 60 per month for an average home in Canada.

Moreover, homeowner's insurance tends to be several times higher than tenant's.

In fact, these extra insurance costs for owning a house can add up to tens of thousands of dollars over the duration of the mortgage loan.

Potential Mortgage Rate Increase

Given the duration of the investment, it might be the case that the lending rates are increased by the time of the mortgage renewal. This is another risk faced by a homeowner (as will be illustrated in the third part of the book, a normalization of interest rates might potentially result in a 35 percent increase in monthly mortgage payments from the current levels), while fluctuations in the interest rates have no impact on tenants.

In order to simplify the illustration, we omit the possibility of an increase in mortgage rates and assume a five-year investment horizon at a fixed mortgage rate.

Example

For the numerical illustration and a real-life representation, a real advertisement of two town houses located at the same address in North York, Ontario, (extracted on the same day in November 2015) is evaluated—one town house is for rent while the other one is for sale. Given the size and the age of the town house complex, the units available for sale and rent are identical in size and amenities.

Note that any two options can be evaluated using the model and the readers are welcome to apply the spreadsheet to conduct analysis of their own options. However, the goal of the exercise presented here is to analyze two most comparable options to ensure that we are comparing apples to apples (size, location, and amenities available under the "buy" option should be the same as under the "rent" option).

Ad specifications are as follows:

Town House for Sale ("Buy" Option)	
Asking Price	$639,000
Living Space	1,500 sq. ft.
Parking	Underground
Property Taxes (2015)	$3,399.24
Monthly Maintenance Fees	$560.90
Town House for Rent ("Rent" Option)	
Monthly Rent:	$2,350
Living Space:	1,500 sq. ft.
Parking:	Underground

The selection was done randomly, and all calculations in the section are for illustrative purposes only. It does not have a tremendous importance which units are selected for this numerical exercise, but it is also important to keep our analysis as close to real-life as possible. Moreover, the model that was prepared for this example can be applied to evaluation of any two options that a potential homeowner is faced with. An Excel spreadsheet with embedded formulas is available for download and the guidelines are available at the end of this section.

In order to prepare a clear set of analysis, we imposed a set of simplifying (but yet realistic) assumptions.

"Buy" Option

For the "buy" option, the assumptions are as follows:

1. The horizon of this investment is five years; after that, the property is assumed to be sold.

2. In accordance with the current regulations, the amount of the required down payment for a home priced above $1 million is 20 percent; otherwise a 5 percent rate is applied for the first $500,000 and a 10 percent rate is applied for the remaining part. In our example, a home is priced at $639,000, and the minimum down payment required is $38,900 ($500,000 at 5 percent, plus $139,000 at 10 percent).

3. An assumed mortgage loan is financed at a fixed rate of 3.50 percent (for your own calculations the rate can be adjusted).

4. The length of the mortgage loan is twenty-five years or three hundred months (this value can also be adjusted when you do your personal calculations).

5. Forgone earnings on the down payment are assumed to be an arbitrary 5 percent per year (the money spent as an initial payment could have been invested in the stock market using passive investment instruments such as a mutual fund or an ETF if the house is rented).

6. At the time of a purchase, a buyer is assumed to incur a fixed cost of $1,500 that includes legal and appraisal fees (a figure provided to me by a mortgage broker).

7. At the time of a purchase, a buyer is also assumed to incur a cost associated with the land transfer tax. The amount of this tax depends on the location of a house (properties located in Toronto are subject to provincial as well as municipal taxes). There are many Web sites that offer calculators that estimate land transfer tax, and probably the most user-friendly Web site is www.ratehub.ca.

8. Our calculations assume that a buyer is purchasing his/her first house and qualifies for a land transfer tax rebate of $5,725.

9. A homeowner is responsible for capital renovation costs, such as exterior painting, roof leakage, plumbing issues, HVAC repair, etc. An arbitrary rate of 0.60 percent of the house price per year is assumed to be incurred by a homeowner.

10. In the consequent years, certain monthly expenditures are assumed to increase at a rate of 2 percent a year (in particular, property taxes, maintenance fees, phone/cable/Internet, capital renovation costs, and home insurance).

Having made these assumptions, we are now ready to prepare a summary of all expenses to be incurred by a potential homeowner (initial, as well as monthly recurring payments).

Option 1: Buy

Summary	Amount
House Price	639,000.00
Down payment	38,900.00
Mortgage Loan	600,100.00
Mortgage Rate	3.50%
Mortgage Length (months)	300

Monthly Expenses in Year 1	
Mortgage	3,004.24
Property Tax	283.27
Mortgage Insurance	72.01
Maintenance Fees	560.90
Phone/Cable/Internet	130.00
Insurance	140.58
Forgone Earnings on Down Payment	162.08
Capital Renovations	319.50
Total	4,672.59

Initial Expenses	
Down Payment	38,900.00
Legal Fees	1,500.00
Land Transfer Tax (after rebate)	11,271.00
Total	51,671.00

"Rent" Option

The "rent" option also has a set of simplifying assumptions:

1. Monthly rent payments of $2,350 are assumed to grow at 2 percent a year, and the same growth rate is applied to phone/cable/Internet and tenant's home insurance expenses.

2. No initial expenses are incurred by a tenant, and maintenance fees are paid by the landlord.

With these assumptions, monthly expenditures are summarized as follows:

Option 2: Rent					
Monthly Expenses	Year 1	Year 2	Year 3	Year 4	Year 5
Rent	2,350.00	2,397.00	2,444.94	2,493.84	2,543.72
Phone/Cable/Internet	130.00	132.60	135.25	137.96	140.72
Insurance	38.75	39.53	40.32	41.12	41.94
Total	2,518.75	2,569.13	2,620.51	2,672.92	2,726.38

Analysis

There are many ways to evaluate these two options, but in order to have a concise, realistic, and understandable set of analysis, the following assumptions are imposed:

1. Calculations are made over a five-year investment horizon, and the house is assumed to be sold and the outstanding mortgage amount paid out at the end of year 5.

2. Present value of the cash flows is calculated using an arbitrary discount rate of 2 percent per year. This is required due to the "time-value-of-money" concept (a dollar in a year from now is worth less than today in a normal economy; I assume it is worth 2 percent less every year). This also enables us to manipulate (add and subtract) all cash flows in today's dollars, since transactions occur every year from now to the end of year 5.

Graphical representation of discounting in our exercise is shown below:

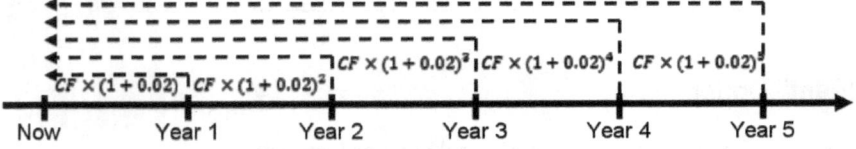

3. The sale of the house is assumed to take place at the end of year 5, and three cases are considered for the change in price relative to the purchase price:

- Case 1: Sale at cost (sale price at the end of year 5 is equal to the purchase price).
- Case 2: Sale with a 15 percent gain (sale price at the end of year 5 is 15 percent higher than the purchase price).
- Case 3: Sale with a 10 percent loss (sale price at the end of year 5 is 10 percent lower than the purchase price).

These cases are all valid and realistic and should not be disregarded by a prospective investor. At the end of this section, we provide guidelines on how to use the spreadsheet with these calculations, and how to make adjustments to calculations when a reader conducts his/her own analysis.

After imposing these assumptions and clarifications, we now have all the tools required for evaluation of the two options—"buy" or "rent." Mathematically, the two equations look as follows:

$$\text{Buy} = IE + \sum CF(Y1) \times (1 + 0.02) + \sum CF(Y2) \times (1 + 0.02)^2 + \sum CF(Y3) \times (1 + 0.02)^3 + \sum CF(Y4) \times (1 + 0.02)^4 + [\sum CF(Y5) - Sale + Mortgage\ Repayment] \times (1 + 0.02)^5$$

Where:

- "IE" is initial expenses incurred "now."

- $\sum CF(Y1)$ is the sum of expenses in year 1, $\sum CF(Y2)$ is the sum of expenses in year 2, etc.

- "Sale" is the sale price of the house at the end of year 5.

- "Mortgage Repayment" is the full repayment of the outstanding balance of the mortgage loan at the end of year 5.

It should be noted that all cash outflows have a positive sign while a cash inflow (sale of the house in year 5) has a negative sign.

Mathematical representation of the "rent" option looks as follows:

$$\text{Rent} = \sum CF(Y1) \times (1 + 0.02) + \sum CF(Y2) \times (1 + 0.02)^2 + \sum CF(Y3) \times (1 + 0.02)^3 + \sum CF(Y4) \times (1 + 0.02)^4 + \sum CF(Y5) \times (1 + 0.02)^5$$

A summary of the cash flows for the two options and their discounted values (present value) are presented in the table below:

	Buy	Present Value "BUY"	Rent	Present Value "RENT"
Today	51,671	51,671	-	-
Year 1	56,071	54,972	30,225	29,632
Year 2	56,415	54,225	30,830	29,632
Year 3	56,766	53,492	31,446	29,632
Year 4	57,125	52,774	32,075	29,632
Year 5	57,490	52,070	32,717	29,632
Case 1: Sale at Cost	(607,050)	(549,824)		
Case 2: Sale with a 15% Gain	(698,108)	(632,297)		
Case 3: Sale with a 10% Loss	(546,345)	(494,841)		
Mortgage Repayment	518,009	469,176		

By adding present values of cash flows for the two options, we are able to simply compare two numbers and derive a conclusion by how much an investor is better off or worse off when renting the town house rather than buying it (note that positive numbers in the table indicate a cash outflow).

	"BUY"	"RENT"	DIFFERENCE ("BUY" minus "RENT")
Case 1: Sale at Cost	238,557	148,162	90,395
Case 2: Sale with a 15% Gain	156,083	148,162	7,921
Case 3: Sale with a 10% Loss	293,539	148,162	145,377

The results of this lengthy numerical exercise indicate that if an individual were to buy the town house in North York for $639,000 rather than to rent it for $2,350 per month and the price is unchanged by the time of the sale at the end of year 5, the investor is worse off by over $90,000.

Moreover, if the market undergoes a 10 percent correction, a homeowner would be in the red by $145,000 (which is an equivalent of more than ten years' worth of savings by an average household).

Even if the housing market continues its growing trend, a 15 percent property appreciation still leaves a homeowner with a loss of $8,000 if the "buy" option is chosen.

In fact, in order for a homeowner to be breakeven (i.e., a scenario when an investor is financially indifferent between buying and renting a house), the price appreciation would be required to be 16.50 percent or $105,500.

It is totally in the hands of a reader to determine if such an appreciation of the house is feasible and whether a potential gain outweighs the potential risks associated with the purchase of the home.

The real estate market (like any other market) is not perfect in nature, and profitable investments are always available for savvy investors. Therefore, careful calculations (similar to the ones provided in the book) might enable a reader who has an option to buy an undervalued house with a price growth potential of 10 percent per year to clearly see the financial benefits of owning a house rather than renting it. However, I would warn readers from assuming that the general housing market growth trend will be similar to the trend seen in the last few years (more on this in the next section of the book).

I believe that the Microsoft Excel spreadsheet developed for this section of the book can be a great tool for a potential homeowner to evaluate and analyze the cost of owning a home, relative to the option of renting it. The box below provides step-by-step guidelines on how to use the spreadsheet for evaluation of any options that involve a decision between buying and renting a house/town house/condo in Canada.

Box 1: Step-by-Step Guidelines to the Spreadsheet

1. Go to this link: **www.bit.ly/DmitryNewmanAnalytics**.

2. Download the spreadsheet: Click on Download (blue button in the top right corner); then click on Direct Download to save the file on your computer.

3. Open Rent vs Buy tab. Only yellow cells require an input, and the workbook is protected from changes of any non-yellow cells. All current values are for the numerical example illustrated in the book. You are welcome to make adjustments to the yellow cells to conduct analysis for your personal "buy" and "rent" options.

4. "House Price" (cell C3) is the listing price of the house being evaluated. The down payment and the amount of the mortgage loan are calculated automatically—for a home priced above $1 million, a rate of 20 percent is applied; for a home priced under $500,000, a 5 percent rate is applied; for a price above $500,000 but under $1 million, a rate of 5 percent is applied for the first $500,000 and a 10 percent rate applied for the remaining part.

5. "Mortgage Rate" (cell C6) and "Mortgage Length" (cell C8) depend on your lender and your credit history; the maximum mortgage length is three hundred months.

6. "Property Tax" (cell C12) for a year is usually posted with a listing; divide this number by 12 and insert into the appropriate cell.

7. "Mortgage Insurance" (cell C13) is calculated automatically and does not require an input: for a home price above $1 million, insurance is not required (due to the down payment requirement of 20 percent); otherwise, the total cost of 3.6 percent of the mortgage loan is assumed.

8. "Maintenance Fees" (cell C14) are also posted with a listing; for a detached house, you might be required to contact a mortgage broker/seller to determine an average cost of house maintenance.

9. "Phone/Cable/Internet" (cell C15) expense depends on a provider and the services; the spreadsheet assumes an equal cost for renting and buying options.

10. "Insurance" (cells C16 and C34) can be determined for both options by filling in an online questionnaire; tenant's insurance tends to be cheaper than homeowner's.

11. "Land Transfer Tax" (cell C26) can be determined by using a calculator http://www.ratehub.ca/land-transfer-tax.

12. "Rent" (cell C32) is the monthly rental fee to be incurred under the "rent" option (including maintenance fees if they are to be paid by a tenant).

13. Open Evaluation tab; all cells except B9 and B10 in this tab are formula-based.

14. Enter expected non-annualized home price growth rates by the end of year 5 for case 2 (cell B9) and case 3 (cell B10).

15. Column G (cells G14 through G16) provides a numerical illustration by how much (in today's dollars), the "buy" option is better or worse than the "rent" option. Positive values in the column G indicate the amount of loss from buying a house relative to renting it. Negative values in the column G indicate the amount of gain from buying the house relative to renting it.

Note: The "Mortgage Amortization Schedule" tab is formula-based and does not require any input. The tab is required to calculate an outstanding balance of the mortgage loan to be repaid at the end of year 5.

As was stated multiple times thus far, profitable investment opportunities exist in any market, but I am under the view that it is more and more challenging to make a profitable investment in real estate in Canada. As was illustrated in this section, just to be breakeven and to be able to cover the cost of homeownership, a 16.5 percent capital appreciation in five years is required to be achieved when buying the town house in North York instead of renting it.

In addition, a homeowner assumes additional risks such as a possibility of a price correction. As was illustrated in our numerical example, a 10 percent price correction will result in a loss of $145,000.

Some readers might conclude that, given the growth in real estate prices in the last three to five years, a 16.50 percent price appreciation of the town house is more than feasible (in fact, some prospective homeowners might estimate a 10 percent appreciation per year), but there is a large number of factors signalling a limited opportunity for growth potential for the housing market in the next five to ten years.

The purpose of the next part of the book is to provide analysis of why the upside potential for housing prices is limited and why potential risks of being a homeowner outweigh the potential benefits.

Housing Market Growth Prospects

C anada's business press of late has been flooded with skeptics that draw similarities of the Canadian housing market and the one experienced in the Unites States in 2008–09 and urge to take short positions on securities that are directly linked to the housing market and warn prospective households of dangers associated with purchase of a home in Canada under current market conditions.

How credible these calls really are?

A severe housing market crash in Canada is highly unlikely, but an upside potential is also very limited. Therefore, careful monitoring of the housing market dynamics should be implemented by potential real estate owners, keeping in mind that it is possible to make a profitable investment decision in a growing market as well as in a stagnating one, but it requires a great deal of knowledge and research.

It strikes me each time I hear overly optimistic remarks about the housing market in Canada—real estate agents aside (their remarks do not strike me at all as they are making a commission from sales), but rather the remarks of financial analysts that forecast an unprecedented growth of the market. And the reasoning that they provide goes like this: "Well, in the last few years, the price of real estate growth was in double digits . . ." or "Um, my aunt bought a condo in 2009, and now it's worth 40 percent more . . . ."

There is one underlying weakness in these statements—they are all historical and not forward-looking.

In fact, I would place these arguments in the "against" column for a homeownership decision as everyone knows that everything comes to an end at some point, including an exceptional double-digit growth of the Canadian housing market. The higher the market climbs, the sharper correction should be expected.

In this section, I provide a list of forward-looking arguments that signal softening of the real estate market in Canada.

Real estate (like any other market) is driven by the forces of supply (how many housing units are offered—new and previously owned) and demand (how many housing units are purchased). Ultimately, the price is determined by the movements in supply and demand.

For instance, if the number of units offered rises (there is a rise in supply), with an unchanged demand, the price falls; similarly, if the number of units purchased falls (there is a fall in demand), with an unchanged supply, the price also falls.

With this basic concept in mind, we can proceed to the analysis of the forces of supply and demand that drove the Canadian housing prices to the level where they are today and what is likely to happen with these forces in the years to come.

Expectations of Excess Supply

One economic metric widely used by analysts for evaluation of the direction of the housing supply is Housing Starts (reported by Statistics Canada on a monthly basis).

On a seasonally adjusted annual rate, average housing starts in the third quarter of 2015 were 213,000 units, which represent a 20,000 increase from the second quarter and nearly a 40,000 increase from the first quarter.[19]

Annual household formation (the number of new households) in Canada is estimated to be around 185,000. Housing Starts below this value will be absorbed by the market and will avoid creation of an excess supply in the long run.

The current rate of 213,000, if persisted in the long run, might become a worrisome sign.

---

[19]   Canada Mortgage and Housing Corporation, *Dwelling Starts (SAAR, Thousands of Units)*, retrieved November 18, 2015, from Haver Analytics database (GM00001@CANADA).

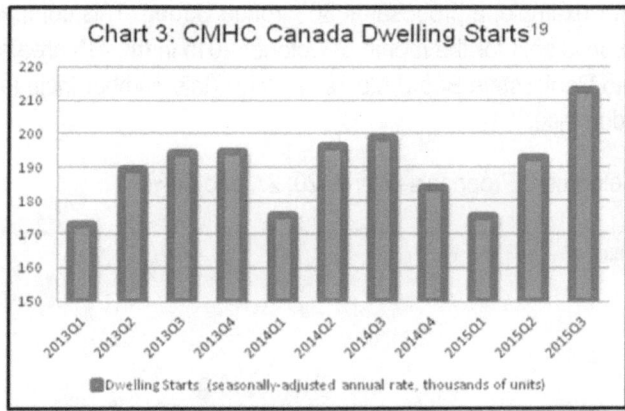

It should be noted, however, that Housing Starts data is volatile in nature, and since the beginning of 2013, Housing Starts averaged 190,000, which seems to be in line with the household formation estimate of 175,000–185,000 and, on its own, the figure does not indicate an excess supply of housing in Canada. The purpose of this illustration is to prove an absence of any supply weakness in the near future.

Additionally, the data only includes housing units that started being constructed. It generally takes several years from a decision to build a condo complex and the start of the development. As such, a substantial number of development projects that were started in 2012–15 (years when housing market prices saw an incredible growth) are not yet included in the Housing Starts data.

There are a limited number of data sources available on aggregate development proposals in Canada (that truly could provide us with the direction of the supply of housing in the long run). We can only monitor such development proposals in some large cities. For example, the city of Toronto has a tool that provides a breakdown of proposals by wards.

The screenshots of the three Toronto central wards (20, 27, and 28) extracted in November of 2015 show three hundred development proposals[20] (which at some point may become housing starts, if approved).

Indeed, some of these projects are small two-story buildings, but some of them are large sixty-story towers that will release over 1,100 condo units into the market once

---

20   City of Toronto, *Development Projects Applications – Wards 20, 27, 27,* accessed November 15, 2015, available from http://app.toronto.ca/DevelopmentApplications/mapSearchSetup. do?action=init.

completed (for example, a proposal at 363 Yonge Street). This compares to only 1,587 condo units sold for the month of October 2015 in the 416 area as reported in the Toronto Real Estate Board Market Watch[21] (this number includes new and existing condo units).

Toronto Development Proposals–Wards 20, 27, and 28 [20]

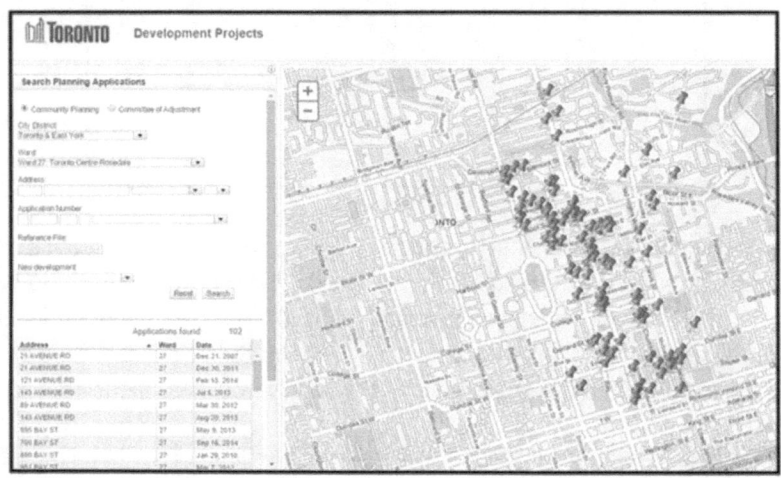

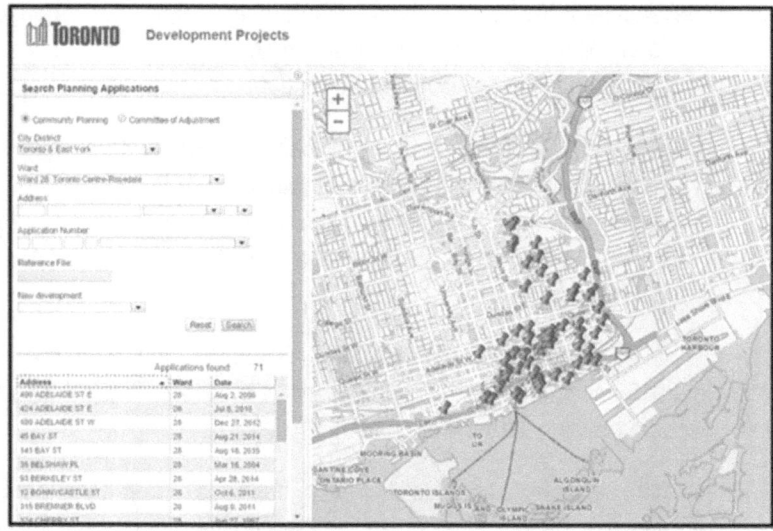

21   Toronto Real Estate Board, *Market Watch* (October 2015), available from http://www.trebhome.
      com/market_news/market_watch/2015/mw1510.pdf.

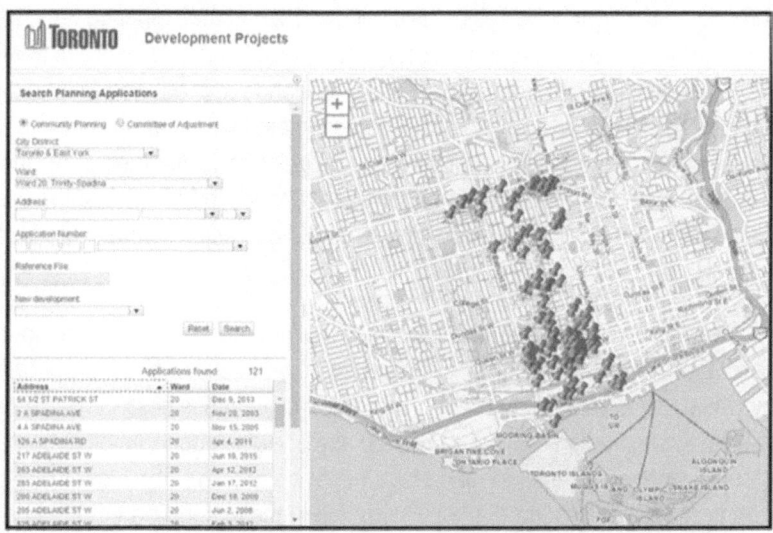

The prospects of a potential excess supply in smaller markets are also highlighted by the government authorities.

The CMHC in the fall of 2015 released an update on the housing market in Canada and warned of signs of an overbuilding in Winnipeg, Saskatoon, and Regina. The agency warned of a possibility of an emergence of an overbuilding of condo units in Toronto, Montreal, and Ottawa.[22]

Given an aggressive construction of multi-family dwellings (condominiums, in particular), as opposed to detached housing, the time and resources required to produce one unit of housing are reduced substantially and responsiveness of supply to an increase in demand is therefore accelerated.

For instance, if there was an upsurge in demand, there will be a corresponding upsurge in the supply of new condominium units, thereby limiting any upside price potential in an uncertain world.

The latest spike in the condominium construction also imposes certain risks and difficulties to be faced in the long run as a large number of downtown condos in Toronto and Vancouver are rented and will have a problem with deferred maintenance (renters are more abusive to common facilities then are owner-occupiers).

---

[22]   Canada Mortgage and Housing Corporation, *Housing Market Assessment* (Fourth Quarter 2015).

Secondly, a condo/town house owner is paying taxes and maintenance fees, which are likely to equal or even exceed rent for a comparable unit. As was illustrated in the second section of the book, a very substantial price appreciation is required to compensate for all the additional expenses associated with homeownership. The owners, in effect, are counting on future capital gains to justify their investments. There is a downside risk to prices, and there are reasons to believe that the upside potential will always be limited, given increased supply responsiveness and a shift toward multiunit dwellings.

Finally, it was reported on numerous occasions that new condominiums are not well-built, and the extensive use of glass exteriors is a "time bomb" in terms of both energy waste and in terms of future replacement/maintenance costs. When making a long-term investment in real estate (especially in a glass condominium unit), it is important to realize that maintenance fees might be growing at a higher rate than just 2 percent as was assumed in the illustration in the second part of the book.

Now, let's turn to the demand side story.

Immigration System Changes

While Canada's adult population is still growing, the data indicates that the year-over-year growth rate has been steadily declining on a national level (according to the Labour Force Information report released by Statistics Canada on monthly basis).

For instance, year-over-year population growth on a national level declined from 1.5 percent in the early 2000s to 1.0 percent in 2015.[23]

---

[23]   Statistics Canada, *Labour Force Information (71-001-X)*, retrieved November 15, 2015, from Haver Analytics (V9L45764@CANADAR).

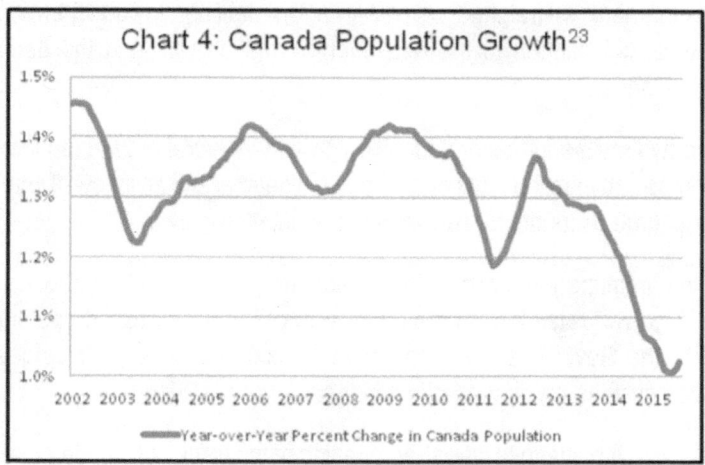

Toronto (second hottest real estate market after Vancouver) had a more drastic slowdown in the year-over-year growth from 2.8 percent in the early 2000s to 1.7 percent in 2015.[24]

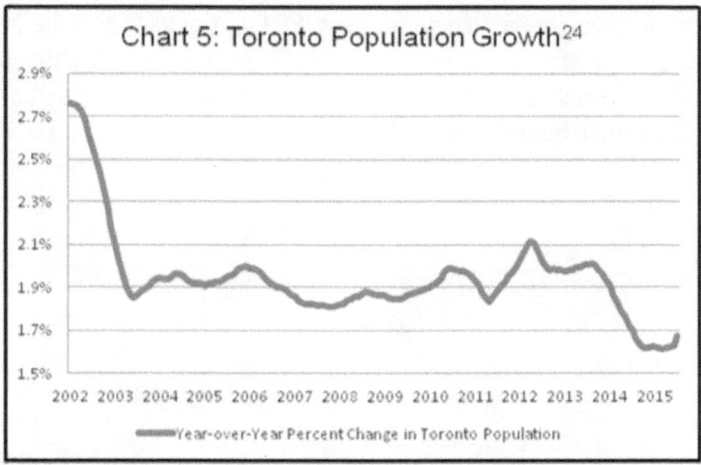

What is particularly worrisome is that a sharp acceleration of the decline in population growth started in 2012 and continued to date.

---

24   Statistics Canada, *Labour Force Information (71-001-X)*, retrieved November 15, 2015, from Haver Analytics (V9L46072@CANADAR).

The question here is straightforward: with a long-lasting slowdown in population growth, what will happen to the household formation rate and the demand for housing in Canada?

There are two main sources of population growth—natural growth (an increase in the difference between the number of births and deaths) and an inflow of immigrants. The later source accounts for two-thirds of population growth.[25]

Welcoming immigration policies have accounted for most of the excessive population growth rates in Canada (relative to other industrialized countries), but since 2014 the Government of Canada implemented a series of changes to the immigration system, which took effect in the summer of 2015.

The purpose of the changes was strengthening of the value of Canada's citizenship, but in reality, the newly implemented laws place Canada at a disadvantaged position in the eyes of prospective foreign immigrants (which are also believed to be the main source of real estate demand growth).

The statistics released by Citizenship and Immigration Canada indicate a sharp 12 percent reduction in permanent resident (PR) visa issuance for the first three months of 2015 relative to the first three months of 2014 (from 76,091 to 67,150 visas). This represents an acceleration of a declining trend with an annual decline in PR visa issuance from 277,000 in 2010 to 256,000 in 2014.[26]

[25] Statistics Canada Population Growth in Canada, *Immigration: Soon to Be Canada's Only Source of Population Growth* (January 25, 2008), accessed November 5, 2015, available from http://www.statcan.gc.ca/pub/91-003-x/2007001/4129907-eng.htm.

[26] Government of Canada, *Business Line - Authorizations and Visas Issued for Permanent Residents (in Persons)*, July 23, 2015, accessed November 5, 2015, available from http://open.canada.ca/data/en/dataset/adc5dff8-b7e7-4abb-ad56-de970e7ab3b9.

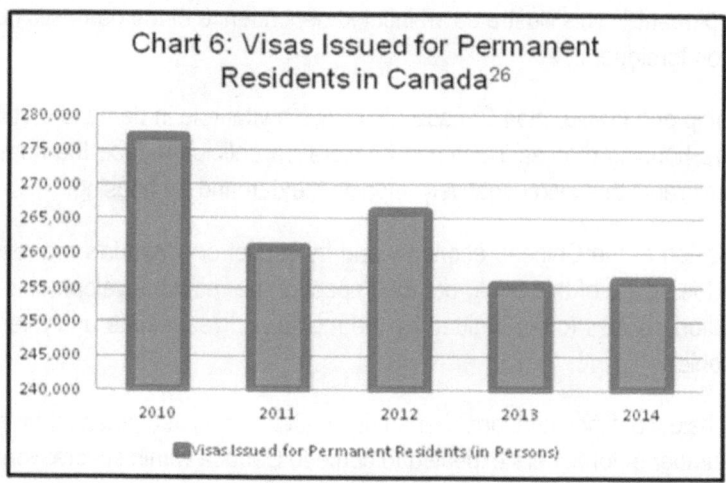

Successful PR holders are soon-to-be Canadian citizens that most certainly impacted population growth in Canada in recent years, which in turn influenced the demand for housing (with a time lag).

It is also important to note that the decline in the number of permanent residents admitted in Canada took place even before the implementation of the stringent immigration policies that, if not reversed, will undercut the number of new immigrants further.

The negative shock on the number of foreigners granted PR status seems to be long-lasting in nature and potentially will continue suppressing the number of new immigrants and thus reducing demand for Canada's housing, given that changes are not reversed.

The results of the negative shock on the number of immigrants and Canada's population growth are only to be seen in 2016–17 and the negative impact on housing demand is only to follow within five to seven years.

There are no reliable government-based sources on the share of foreign/recent immigrants' ownership in Canada's real estate market and analysts are forced to rely on private surveys to get some idea on the importance of the foreign demand for the real estate market in Canada.

Vice president of operations at Macdonald Realty, Jonathan Cooper, determined that 70 percent buyers for properties sold for more than $3 million came from China, based on the sales in 2014. For homes priced between $1 and $3 million, the share was 21 percent.[27] This illustrates an inflated dependence of the domestic housing market on foreigners.

Citizenship and Immigration Canada also plays a vital role in demand stability for Canada's housing market. Tightened immigration policies reduce the number of new immigrants that also negatively impacts the demand for housing.

A discussion of the Chinese economy and its impact on Canada's real estate is beyond the scope of this book, but the impact of the recent developments in the immigration policies (often omitted by the media and real estate analysts) might be valuable.

The list below outlines changes that are indicative of a limited potential for growth in the number of foreigners expected to come to Canada within several years.

Termination of the Federal Immigrant Investor and Entrepreneurs Program

Until February 11, 2014, wealthy foreigners were able to become permanent residents of Canada by making a long-term investment in the Canadian economy. Roughly 2 to 3 percent of 250,000 immigrants per year that come to Canada used this immigration channel, so the number is not overwhelmingly large, but this group of immigrants has the resources for influencing real estate market (either in a form of making a purchase of a place of residence or making real estate investments).

Instead, an Immigrant Investor Venture Capital Fund pilot project has been launched in 2015 that selects only sixty applicants (on a first come, first served basis) and will require a $2 million investment from the selected participants. This will not be enough to cover the real estate demand created by wealthy foreigners under the investor program.

---

[27]   Jim Middlemiss, *Canada's Ever Growing Housing Bubble: As Alberta's Market Tumbles, the Rest of the Country Wonders Who's Next* (The Financial Post Magazine, September 15, 2015), accessed December 5, 2015, available from http://business.financialpost.com/news/economy/ canadas-ever-growing-housing-bubble-as-albertas-market-tumbles-the-rest-of-the-country-wonders-whos-next.

Changes to the Permanent Residence Application (for Foreigners with Canadian Experience)

Prior to the changes that came in effect in June of 2015, there was a simplified program that enabled foreigners that landed a skilled or semiskilled full-time employment in almost any industry in Canada to become permanent residents within one year. This channel was particularly useful for international students that are granted an open work permit for every year of schooling (up to three years) and are able to expand a job search to multiple industries in order to gain the experience needed for immigration.

With the newly implemented changes, the Government of Canada provides an assessment and determines if a candidate is employed in an industry that has a shortage of skilled workers (i.e., the assessment is done after a potential immigrant was employed for at least a year at a job that may or may not qualify for immigration purposes).

This change provides protection to Canada's labor market, but it also creates a high degree of uncertainty to potential immigrants and reduces the attractiveness of Canada among international students whose goal is to immigrate and build a life in Canada.

Increase in Citizenship Wait Times

Once a candidate becomes a permanent resident, he/she is required to wait for four years (as opposed to three years prior to June 2015) before submitting an application for a Canadian passport.

Previously, permanent residents were able to reduce their wait time by up to one year by accounting for the time they spent in Canada before gaining a permanent resident status. Ultimately, for these foreigners, the wait times for a Canadian passport increased from two to four years.

Canada has also been a popular destination for international students that come to the country at an early age, pay international students fees (usually triple the amount of the tuition fees paid by domestic students), and end up immigrating after providing a proof of stable employment and earnings.

In addition to tightening of immigration laws to these individuals (an increase in wait times for a citizenship from two to four years and an uncertainty when applying for a permanent resident status), the cost of education also increased dramatically.

For example, a standard bachelor of commerce program at the University of Toronto cost roughly $45,000 a year for a student enrolling into the program in 2015 as opposed to $30,000 a year for a student enrolling into the program in 2010 (this is a 50 percent increase in just five years). In no way this discussion criticizes the immigration changes implemented by the Canadian government; the whole point is to forecast an expected inflow of immigrants that potentially influenced Canada's real estate in the last decade.

While the possibility of seeing a plunge in housing demand due to the immigration changes is minimal, if the 12 percent decline in PR visa issuance we saw in the first quarter of 2015 relative to the first quarter of 2014 persists throughout the year, it will be difficult to see an increase in housing demand from foreigners in the years to come, which can also place a downward pressure on housing prices.

A Limited Downside Potential for Mortgage Rates

Interest rates are at historically lowest level and with the Bank of Canada overnight rate at 0.50 percent by the end of 2015, a substantial reduction of rates offered by mortgage lenders is unlikely.

The Bank of Canada rate has been cut twice in 2015 to address the softness in the Canadian economy from the plunge in oil prices in mid-2014. While the Federal Reserve of America is on a path to policy normalization cycle, a further rate cut by the Bank of Canada remains unlikely, unless the economic climate in Canada deteriorates.

Furthermore, a desire by the Fed to raise rates prove a point that the near-zero interest rates is not a new norm.

As chart 7 illustrates, the current Bank of Canada overnight rate at 0.50 percent is abnormal, and it can be assumed that the normalization of the rate will commence as soon as the economy stabilizes from the oil price plunge.

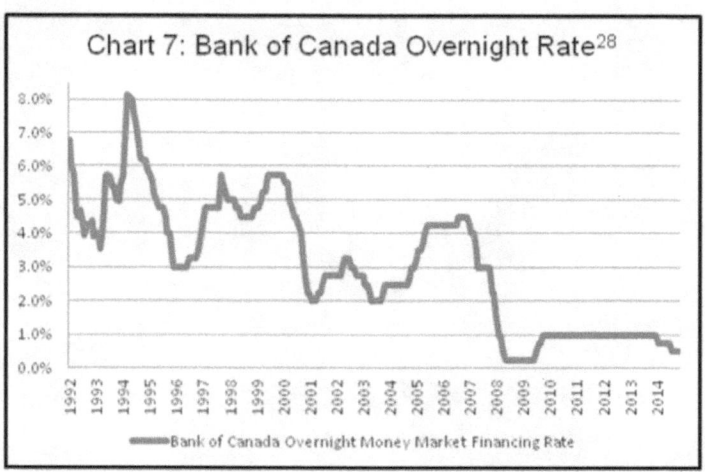

The average Bank of Canada overnight rate for the period from 1993 to 2007 was 4.1 percent,[28] which is 360 basis points higher than the current rate.

A normalization of the overnight rate will result in an increase in mortgage rates that followed the overnight Bank of Canada rate and slid from an average of 7.2 percent during the period from 1993 to 2007 to 3.7 percent in July of 2015,[29] which is historically lowest level (based on the data provided by the Canada Mortgage and Housing Corporation on a five-year conventional fixed mortgage lending rate).

---

[28]   Bank of Canada, *Overnight Money Market Financing Rate*, retrieved November 10, 2015, from Haver Analytics database (B156RD@CANADA).

[29]   Canada Mortgage and Housing Corporation, *Canada: Conventional Mortgage Lending Rate: Five Year Term (%)*, retrieved August 15, 2015, from Haver Analytics database (DP00001@ CANADA).

Chart 8: CMHC Conventional Fixed Mortgage Rate[29]

While a return to the historical norms in mortgage rates cannot be expected in the next few years, housing investments are twenty to twenty-five years long, and it might be expected to have a rate increase to a more sustainable level of 5–7 percent throughout duration of a mortgage loan started in 2015.

The difference between a 7.2 percent and a 3.7 percent mortgage rate might not feel substantial, but the impact on monthly payments is, in fact, significant (especially for households that spend the largest portion of their disposable income on mortgage payments).

For instance, a 350 basis point increase in mortgage rates results in an astonishing 40 percent increase in monthly mortgage payments. For example, monthly payments on a $500,000, twenty-five-year mortgage loan will increase from $2,550 to $3,560 if the mortgage rate is raised from 3.7 percent to 7.2 percent.

Below is the table that illustrates sensitivity of monthly payments on this hypothetical mortgage loan to changes in interest rates, all other things unchanged:

Interest Rate	Monthly Payment	Percent Increase
3.50%	$2,496.36	
4.50%	$2,767.37	+10.9%
5.50%	$3,051.96	+10.3%
6.50%	$3,349.12	+9.8%
7.50%	$3,657.78	+9.2%

This is particularly risky for households that allocate 50 percent or more of their income on mortgage payments, property taxes, and maintenance fees. With no ability to save money due to substantial outflows on mortgage payments and a high degree of vulnerability from a job loss, there is a tremendous risk of housing market decline in case of a mild economic recession that will result in a rise of unemployment and a rate of foreclosures that, in turn, will drive the price of housing down.

Some analysts rely on the Bank of Canada's index for a measure of housing affordability that portrays present housing at one of the most affordable level in history—at 0.31 as of the first quarter of 2015 compared to the average of 0.39 in 1980s and 0.34 in 1990s.[30]

The index estimates the share of housing-related expenses out of disposable income. It should not come as a surprise that the latest improvement in the measure is almost fully attributed to the historically lowest mortgage rates which are 340 basis points lower than the prerecessionary level and might potentially rise by 200–300 basis points within several years which will increase housing-related expenses for homeowners by a third, making housing most unaffordable since 1980s, all other things being equal.

Mr. Thomas Binet of Desjardins in his Economic Viewpoint (May 26, 2014) determined that "each 25-basis-point increase in Canada's key rate triggers a 0.6

30   Bank of Canada, *Housing Affordability Index*, accessed November 5, 2015, available from http://credit.bankofcanada.ca/financialconditions.

percent decline in property prices after four years, versus the original equilibrium level, all things being equal."[31] The study concludes that an increase in interest rates will have a negative impact on the housing market.

A numerical implication of an interest rate increase on home prices should not be viewed as of a tremendous significance. What most importantly I would like my readers to bring with them after reading this section is that a rise in interest rates will inevitably take place, which might potentially cause a rise in monthly mortgage payments by 20–30 percent. Families considering a purchase of a home under current market conditions should carefully weigh their ability to tolerate such a rise in monthly payments without a negative impact on their lifestyle and their ability to save for retirement.

Macroeconomic Environment in Canada

Oil Price Impact

Canada's economy was hit hard by the plunge in oil prices (natural resources sector accounts for nearly 20 percent of the economy and is responsible for employment of 1.8 million of Canadians while the energy sector alone accounts for 10 percent of the economy).[32]

As chart 10 illustrates, the plunge in oil prices that commenced in the summer of 2014 (when the price of the West Texas Intermediate or WTI oil brand was near 105 dollars per barrel) had several attempts to recover in 2015 but, to date (December 2015), remains below the $40 per barrel mark.

A similar slump in oil prices took place in 2008 (when oil prices collapsed from $140 per barrel to $40 per barrel within a few months). The collapse was sharp,

---

[31]   Thomas Binet, *Economic Viewpoint*, Desjardins Economic Studies (May 26, 2014), accessed November 20, 2015, available from https://www.desjardins.com/ressources/pdf/pv140526-e. pdf?resVer=1401111569000.

[32]   Statistics Canada, *Key Facts and Figures on the Natural Resources Sector* (July 2015), accessed November 20, 2015, available from http://www.nrcan.gc.ca/publications/ key-facts/16013.

but the recovery was also drastic and the oil price above the $60 per barrel mark was achieved within a year after the collapse.[33]

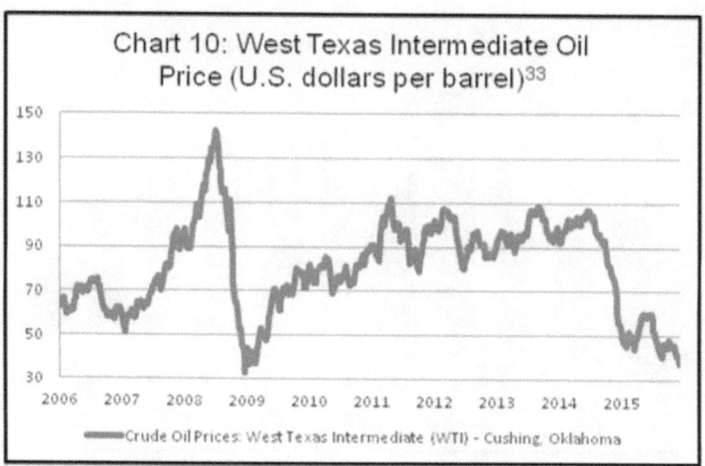

Chart 10: West Texas Intermediate Oil Price (U.S. dollars per barrel)[33]

Currently, a year and a half has passed since the start of the price decline, but the oil price remains at its lowest level.

This resulted in an unpleasant, to say the least, impact on the domestic economy. In fact, during the first half of the year, the Canadian economy fell into technical recession due to the 0.2 percent and 0.1 percent quarter-over-quarter GDP contraction in the first quarter and the second quarter of 2015, respectively. A technical recession implies two consecutive quarters of negative GDP growth; the official bodies responsible for announcement of a recession did not declare it due to certain strength in the labor market as well as the expectations of an economic growth from an expansionary monetary policy implemented by the Bank of Canada in a form of a rate cut in January and June of 2015.

Regardless of the technicalities and the classification, the current economic downturn is evident as the annual GDP growth nearly halved in 2015 relative to the growth seen in 2013 and 2014: 1.2 percent and 1.1 percent annual growth in

---

[33]   US Energy Information Administration, *Crude Oil Prices: West Texas Intermediate (WTI) - Cushing, Oklahoma*, retrieved on December 12, 2015, from the Federal Reserve of St. Louis Economic Data (DCOILWTICO), available from https://research.stlouisfed.org/fred2/series/DCOILWTICO/downloaddata.

the second and the third quarters of 2015, respectively, as opposed to the average growth rate of 2.3 percent in 2013–14.[34]

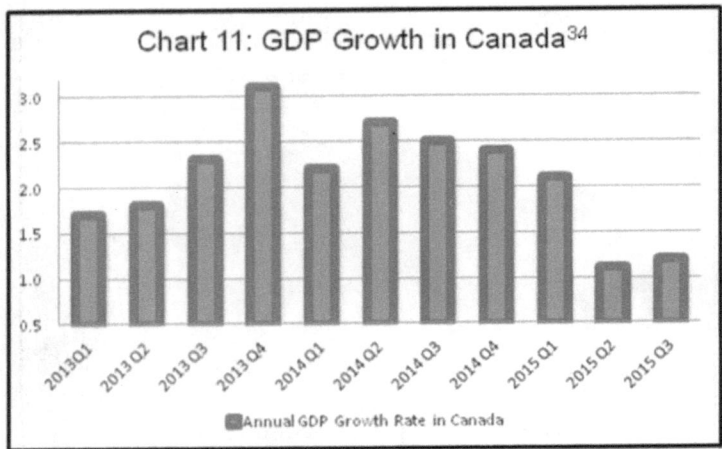

Chart 11: GDP Growth in Canada[34]

While this economic downturn does not have an evidently negative impact on the Canadian real estate market thus far, the big question is what will be the impact if the economic downturn turns out to be long-lasting.

One extreme scenario presented by Canada Mortgage and Housing Corporation chief, Evan Siddall, at the end of November 2015, indicated that a decline of oil prices to the level of $35 per barrel for a duration of five years might trigger unemployment level of 12.5 percent and a collapse of housing prices by 26 percent.[35]

If we go back to the numerical exercise in the second part of the book and apply a 26 percent decline, all other things unchanged, an investor that decides to buy a home instead of renting, he/she would be worse off by $233,000 by the end of year 5—the loss that not only impacts the quality of life of a household during the working years but possibly the retirement years.

Admittedly, this scenario described by the CMHC chief is extreme, but how realistic is it? Did we have occasions in history when the price of oil was suppressed for extended periods of time?

34   Statistics Canada, *Table 380-0064 - Gross Domestic Product, Expenditure-Based, Quarterly (Dollars Unless Otherwise Noted)*, CANSIM database, accessed December 5, 2015.

35   "House Prices Could Fall 26% If Oil Hits $35 and Stays for 5 Years: CMHC," CBC News Business (December 1, 2015), accessed December 5, 2015, available from: http://www.cbc.ca/news/business/cmhc-low-oil-1.3345304.

Indeed, the most recent occurrence of an extended oil price decline was just three decades ago when the WTI oil price plunged from over $30 per barrel at the end of 1985 to $10 per barrel by mid-1986 and remained in the range of $15–20 until mid-1990.[36]

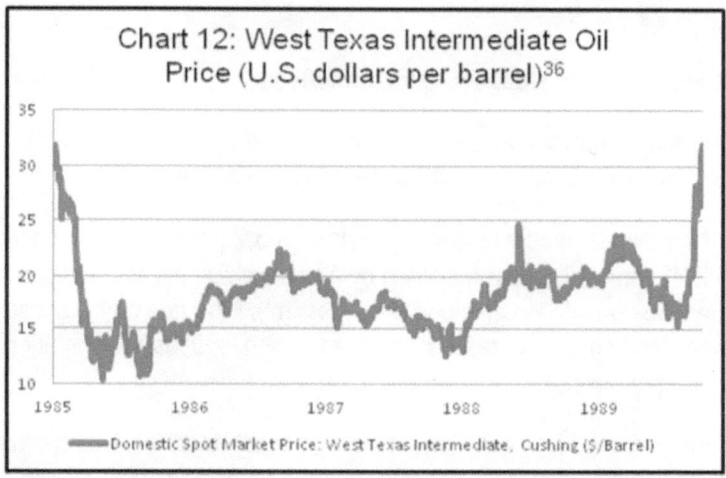

Therefore, to answer the question on how realistic it is to have oil prices halved for an extended period of time, we can certainly say, it is quite realistic.

It should also be noted that Canada's oil dependency in 1980s was substantially weaker than in 2015. The "savior" of the Canadian economy during the oil crisis three decades ago was manufacturing (shortfalls in Alberta's economy were filled by a surge in Ontario's manufacturing). Nowadays, the manufacturing sector in Canada is not at its prime, and its contribution to GDP was nearly halved over the course of the last two decades. As such, Canada's dependency on the energy sector is at the unprecedented levels.

The CMHC provided an even more extreme scenario assuming a widespread worldwide deflation (falling prices) that ultimately suppresses business investment and consumer spending on durable goods (this tendency is on a watch list of many central banks, including the Bank of Canada, the Bank of Japan, the European Central Bank, and the Federal Reserve of the United States). The CMHC estimates

---

36   Energy Information Administration/Chicago Mercantile Exchange, *Domestic Spot Market Price: West Texas Intermediate, Cushing ($/Barrel)*, retrieved August 15, 2015, from Haver Analytics (PZTEXA@DAILY).

a rise in Canada's unemployment rate to 16 percent and a housing price collapse of 44 percent under this scenario.[37]

From our numerical exercise, it follows that a 44 percent plunge in home prices would lead to a hypothetical loss of $332,000 over the period of five years.

Record-High Level of Household Indebtedness

One other major macroeconomic theme that elevates risks for Canada's housing market is household income growth and indebtedness levels.

The average annual median income growth was 3.2 percent for the period from 2000 to 2013 (primarily skewed upward by Alberta where the average growth was 4.5 percent; the growth in Ontario was 2.3 percent),[38] the rate that is not sufficient to compensate for growth in real estate prices, which reduces housing affordability for an average household.

During this phase of historically lowest global interest rates, it is intuitive to expect a growth in indebtedness of households that take advantage of the low cost of debt servicing and purchase durable household items, cars, and housing. However, more and more analysts and policymakers express concerns over an acceleration of the level of indebtedness of Canada's households in the recent years.

Statistics Canada reported that the debt to disposable income ratio hit an all-time high of 167 percent in the second quarter of 2015 (from 164 percent just a year earlier), which was primarily fuelled by the Bank of Canada rate cuts that took place in January and June of 2015.

Similarly, household credit market debt to disposable income ratio hit an all-time high level of 165 percent, which is nearly double the ratio of 85 percent recorded in 1990.[39]

[37] "House Prices Could Fall 26% If Oil Hits $35 and Stays for 5 Years: CMHC," CBC News Business (December 1, 2015), accessed December 5, 2015, available from http://www.cbc.ca/news/business/cmhc-low-oil-1.3345304.

[38] Statistics Canada, *Table 111-0009 - Family Characteristics, Summary, Annual (Number Unless Otherwise Noted)*, CANSIM database, accessed August 20, 2015.

[39] Statistics Canada, *Table - 378-0123 - Households and Non-Profit Institutions Serving Household Sector Indicators – Market Value*, retrieved November 15, 2015, from Haver Analytics (V6H98064@CANADA).

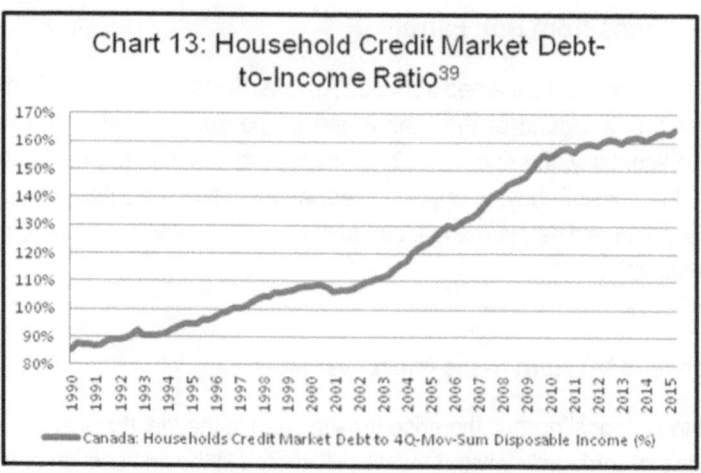

Chart 13: Household Credit Market Debt-to-Income Ratio[39]

Some argue that such an elevated level of household indebtedness is not something to worry about. And indeed, it is not a worrisome sign when market value of household assets also increased: most of the borrowing by households was spent on housing, homeownership rate increased, and the value of household assets increased in tandem with the debt level.

However, in the context of inflated home prices, a high probability of home price moderation and the historically lowest level of interest rates, a record high level of household indebtedness should be closely monitored by policymakers and classified as one of the main risks to stability of the financial system in Canada.

It is clear that currently, Canada does not undergo a period of an economic boom (far from it, in fact). This economic weakness, combined with a plunge and uncertainty in the oil market and an unprecedented level of household indebtedness, inflates risks associated with homeownership in Canada by a household with an average level of income.

The purpose of the discussion on the topic of macroeconomics was not to urge government authorities to address the issues related to household indebtedness and manufacturing industry reforms but rather to inform potential homeowners of the risks and difficulties to be faced by the real estate market in the years to come.

Some Lessons from Bob Farrell

A valuable lesson can be learned from Bob Farrell's "10 Market Rules to Remember." (Bob Farrell is a legend of the Wall Street in the second half of the twentieth century.) Essentially, the rules enable an investor to evaluate market bubbles and to determine possible buying opportunities. Almost all of the rules are applicable to the Canadian real estate market, and in this section, we will assess some of Mr. Farrell's rules:[40]

"Markets tend to return to the mean over time"

Relative to historical norms, the price growth seen in the last three to five years in Canada is extraordinarily inflated. As was illustrated in the first section of the book, the intuition behind homeownership relative to renting for middle-class families is expectations of capital gains rather than cost savings (otherwise, it is not quite evident as to why a family would be willing to spend extra $100,000 over the period of five years when owning a town house in North York, given an unchanged price level).

Once all market forces, such as a mortgage rate rise, population growth moderation with tightened immigration policies, a release of development projects started in 2012–15 to the market, a return to historically sustainable level of housing prices growth in Canada is inevitable.

"There are no new eras—excesses are never permanent"

The only thing we can be certain about is that everything comes to an end. It is hard to believe that anyone related to or interested in Canada's real estate market has any doubts that the market experiences excessive growth. Some might believe that the growth is justified; others might believe that the growth is artificially inflated and expecting a major correction once the forces ease. Regardless of the views, based on this rule, it should be evident that the end to the excessive price growth will come to an end at some point.

---

[40]   Aryeh Katz, "10 Timeless Rules for Investors," Investopedia, accessed November 20, 2015, available from http://www.investopedia.com/articles/fundamental-analysis/09/market-investor-axioms.asp.

The question that prospective owners should ask themselves is whether the moderation in home price growth will be sufficient to outweigh the risks and extra costs of owning a home.

"The public buys the most at the top and the least at the bottom"

A so-called herd behavior concept in behavioral finance states that people tend to mimic behavior of the crowd, regardless of if an action is rational or irrational.

Real estate agents proudly report an increase in home sales every month and more and more people try to become homeowners at any cost (a behavior primarily driven by expectations of the continuing rise of the real estate market).

As we learned from the Housing Market Environment Overview section, more than a quarter of first homebuyers either borrows or receives as a gift financing for the minimum down payment. These are the buyers that are not able to save $20,000–30,000 for a down payment, and I have doubts that these individuals have a clear understanding of consequences of homeownership and the risks associated with it.

As was illustrated in our numerical example, no major correction in home prices is needed for homeowners to become financially worse off relative to households that choose to rent a home.

"Fear and greed are stronger than long-term resolve"

The fear of a possible loss in case of missing an opportunity to enter the market at current prices and the feeling of greed when seeing current homeowners earning hefty paper profits on their homes might overshadow the long-term goals and objectives of many families and result in an absence of proper analysis of the market conditions, personal finances, and options.

Currently, a lack of patience and a desire to become a homeowner at any cost is probably the worst attitude that a household can have when it comes to making a decision to buy or to rent a home.

**"When all the experts and forecasts agree,
something else is going to happen"**

Before starting to write this book, I had at least a few dozen of extremely lengthy debates with prospective middle-class homeowners, university professors, wealthy residential real estate investors, multiple real estate brokers, and all of these individuals (outside of one University of Toronto professor) have one thing in common—they all state that the housing market is currently expensive and possibly unaffordable, but buying a house is a no-loss investment.

They claim that the only obstacle is to raise a minimum down payment and to have sufficient income to qualify for a mortgage loan, without any questioning of growth prospects of the housing market.

When asked why they think this is a no-loss investment opportunity, almost everyone states that renting a house is like "wasting money," as opposed to paying mortgage when you actually create equity.

These statements do not include into consideration the fact that even at one of the historically lowest mortgage rates of 3.50 percent, a monthly mortgage payment includes 50 percent or more of interest in the first sixty-six out of three hundred months. And at an annual mortgage rate of 5.50 percent, the first 151 out of three hundred monthly payments include 50 percent or more of interest.

Another point brought up by universally everyone I had a conversation with is that in the last month (quarter, year, three years), house prices advanced in double digits. This statement is not forward-looking, and most of people fail to understand the reasons why housing prices in Canada are experiencing such a tremendous growth and, most importantly, what is the outlook on these forces in the long run.

One important lesson I would like my readers to take from this book is this: the minute you find yourself surrounded by real estate bears talking about real estate bubble/collapse, it will be a great time to buy a house! The opposite is also true—the minute you find yourself in a room full of real estate bulls, it's time to escape from the market.

Thus far the vast majority of people I have a discussion on the topic of home prices in Canada are stubbornly bullish. This is how I know that I am on the right track!

Final Word

To summarize, an upward potential for Canada's housing market is very limited, but "a bubble burst" of Canada's real estate market is too big of a statement under current market conditions.

Only a truly magnificent economic shock associated with a rapid reduction in employment is able to result in a sharp housing price correction. But this outcome is unlikely, given a relatively resilient response of the Canadian economy to the plunge in oil prices to date.

While Canada almost fully exhausted its economic stimulus using monetary policy channels, the newly elected federal government proposed an extensive fiscal policy stimulus that should ensure economic growth despite a decline in oil prices, which in turn should boost employment and avoid a sharp economic decline.

I would not call for a meltdown of the lending institutions in Canada (similar to the one seen in the United States in the fall of 2008) either. The reasons for sustainability of the financial institutions are their conservative approach (insignificant number of subprime mortgage loans), a high degree of regulations administered by the Government of Canada, and a lender's protection reinforced by the mandatory mortgage insurance on loans with a down payment of under 20 percent.

While it is clear that a housing/financial/economic crash caused by the overheated real estate market is unlikely, a discussion of financial sense of purchasing a house by an average household at market prices rather than renting it, is a tremendous topic and a careful consideration should be given before making such an important decision that might hold a family back for decades (if a price correction takes place).

Moderation of home prices in Canada is inevitable. Moderate price growth will not be sufficient to compensate for the risks and extra costs associated with homeownership.

A risk-reward relationship has been and always will be the key in assessment of any types of investments (the higher return an investor is aiming to achieve, the higher risk he/she is expected to undertake). An abnormal home price growth in Canada with supposedly limited risks in buying a home (assumed by many) violates this risk-reward relationship. There is no such thing as sustainably high returns with low risks in markets with low barriers of entry. Buying a home under current market conditions is a high-risk investment that has a potential of substantial losses.

Just ten years ago, it seemed like a rational choice in the United States to buy and flip houses. Until the end of 2008, this looked like a simple and riskless option to get wealthy. But with the housing crisis, millions of people suffered financially and to this date are not able to repay the debts associated with the unfortunate decision to buy a home in 2006–07.

Homeownership nowadays is a luxury, like buying an expensive piece of clothing. I can't blame people buying expensive clothes (we only live once after all), but before you make such a purchase, it might be a good idea to ask yourself if you can truly afford it.

Hopefully, my book simplifies this assessment process.

ABOUT THE AUTHOR

Dmitry Newman is a University of Toronto graduate and a Bay Street professional with a passion for investments, personal finance advisory, and macroeconomic analysis. He is a founder of a private consulting venture, Dmitry Newman Analytics, that undertakes a unique approach and provides commentary and analysis on global, national, and regional economic trends to help serve readers' business and financial needs.

The author takes pride in writing extensive research papers and commentaries on topics of Canada's retirement income system, international finance, global investment opportunities, and real estate market.

INDEX